Coal Not Dole

Memories of the 1984/85 miners' str
National Union of Mineworkers (Scotlan
STRIKE: Fighting for our Comr.

Compiled by Guthrie Hutton

Arthur Scargill marching along Glaisnock Street, Cumnock, to a rally in June 1984.
Picture courtesy of the *Cumnock Chronicle*

When Arthur Scargill was here for a rally . . . it was big, there were about 10,000 folk at it
. . . they got support from all over Scotland because Arthur was there – I don't think
Cumnock has seen anything like that before – massive!
Bert Smith, Ayrshire.

© Guthrie Hutton 2005
First published in the United Kingdom, 2005,
by Stenlake Publishing Ltd.
Telephone: 01290 551122
Printed by Cordfall Ltd., Glasgow, G21 2QA

ISBN 1 84033 329 4

**The publishers regret that they cannot supply
copies of any pictures featured in this book.**

Foreword

This book, augmented with additional text and pictures, is based on an exhibition, 'STRIKE: Fighting for our Communities', which was set up to commemorate the twentieth anniversary of the Miners' Strike of March 1984 – March 1985. The exhibition was staged for the National Union of Mineworkers (Scotland Area) by the Scottish Mining Museum. It opened in March 2004 and, after an initial period of display at the museum, toured mining-related venues throughout the country.

The National Union of Mineworkers (Scotland Area), the Scottish Mining Museum, the author and the publisher would like to thank the following people for their help in compiling the story both for the exhibition and this book: Eric Clarke, Barney Menzies, Margaret Wegg, Tom Canavan, Bill Ferns, Ian Robb, Elizabeth Marshall, Bert Smith, Neil Valentine, James Hogg, Roberta Black, Ian McAlpine, David McArthur, Duncan 'Spud' Porterfield, Bobby Clelland, Gordon Rodger, Margaret Conners, Liz Paterson, Andrew Stark, Pat Rattray, Cath Cunningham, Margo Russell, David Hamilton MP, Jean Hamilton, Alex Bennett, Tom Coulter, Sam Cowie, David Carruthers, William Muir, John Gillon, Jim Tierney, John McCormack, Jim Douglas, Kay McNamara, Andy Young, Nicky Wilson.

The pictures credited to Fife Mining Archives were taken by John Beal, who donated them to this fine local collection. It is housed in Kinglassie and is open from March to October, Monday to Friday 12.30–3.00. For further information contact the Curator: tel: 01592 753731.

The Scottish Mining Museum houses Scotland's national mining collection and can be contacted or visited at:

The Scottish Mining Museum
Lady Victoria Colliery
Newtongrange, Midlothian
EH22 4QN
Tel: 0131 663 7519
e-mail: enquiries@scottishminingmuseum.org
www.scottishminingmuseum.com

Killoch: one of the new pits begun in the 1950s that had held such promise for the future.

Setting the scene

When the coal industry was nationalised in 1947 hopes were high that lengthy miners' strikes had been consigned to history, but disputes broke out as the National Coal Board (NCB) adapted to the 20th century's changing demands . . .

1955 Peak of post-war output: 850 pits produce 225 million tons.

1970 Fewer than 300 pits left: output 135 million tons.

1970 Conservatives win general election: Edward Heath is the Prime Minister.

1971 NUM elects Joe Gormley as President, narrowly beating Scotland's Mick McGahey.

1972 First national miners' strike since 1926 – Union breaks Government pay policy and Arthur Scargill achieves national prominence leading mass pickets.

1974 Further industrial action by miners provokes Heath to call a general election on the issue of 'Who governs Britain?'. He loses!

The 1984 strike was politically motivated, by the government, they had it organised [to make up for] the humiliations of 1972 and 1974.   *Eric Clarke, Midlothian.*

It was Thatcher's revenge for 1972 and 1974.   *David McArthur, Fife.*

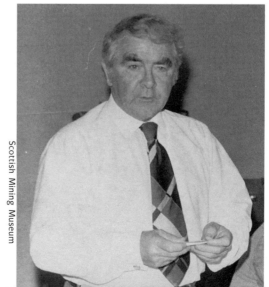

Joe Gormley, who led the union through the strikes of 1972 and 1974.

Mick McGahey who, under NUM rules, was too old to stand for President in 1981, remained the union's national Vice-President and Scottish President throughout the strike.

Countdown to conflict

In 1979, following a period of widespread industrial unrest known as 'The Winter of Discontent', the Conservatives regained power with Margaret Thatcher as Prime Minister. Her government set out to curb the power of the unions generally, and specifically to restructure the nationalised coal industry.

1980 Coal Industry Act: the NCB to become self-supporting by 1983/84.

1981 The NUM threatens industrial action over plans to cut uneconomic capacity: the Government backs off and pumps money into the industry.

1981 Joe Gormley retires as NUM President and is succeeded by Arthur Scargill.

1983 General Election: Margaret Thatcher re-elected Prime Minister.

1983 Scots/American Ian MacGregor appointed NCB Chairman.

The NCB continued to close pits through the early 1980s. In Scotland these cuts were rapid and deep:

1981 Bedlay (near Chryston).

1981 Lady Victoria (Newtongrange).

1982 Kinneil (Bo'ness).

1983 Cardowan (near Stepps).

1983 Highhouse (Auchinleck).

1983 Sorn (near Cumnock).

1984 Bogside (near Longannet).

1984 Closure of Polmaise, Fallin, proposed: a local strike starts on 21 February.

Polmaise Colliery: its proposed closure gave impetus to the strike in Scotland.

Scottish Mining Museum

They were determined to close Polmaise down, we would have been on our own, nobody to back us.

John McCormack, Polmaise.

It was all to do with Thatcher getting rid of trade unions . . . if you can hammer the NUM, nobody else will stand up to you.

David McArthur, Fife.

In the 1980s Margaret Thatcher made it quite clear that at some point or other she would have to pick her ground. She took us on in 1981, but wasn't prepared and backed off . . . I thought then we had a problem. *David Hamilton MP, Midlothian.*

Mrs Thatcher . . . prepared it all, stockpiled coal, changed the delivery of coal to owner drivers, individuals with a mortgage for their lorry instead of big companies, organised the police into a national force and gave them a huge rise in wages, as well as giving wage rises to police judges and the military.

Eric Clarke, Midlothian.

Prior to the big strike, Seafield was on strike, Killoch and Polkemmet were on strike, Monktonhall had been on strike for weeks and other pits were on short periods, and I think the only one that wasn't on strike was Bilston, so they all had problems.

Alex Bennett, Midlothian.

> "... a nuclear programme would have the advantage of removing a substantial portion of electricity production from the dangers of disruption by industrial action by coal miners or transport workers ..."
>
> From the leaked minutes of a Cabinet meeting, Downing St., 29 October 1979

Reproduced courtesy of Paul Morton of Hot Frog Graphics, and Leeds Postcards

Pickets confront a coal-laden lorry.
Picture courtesy of *The Scotsman*. www.scotsman.com

'Here we go, here we go, here we go'

The announcement, on 1 March, that Cortonwood Colliery in Yorkshire was to close sparked a local strike which the NUM Executive backed by declaring a national strike. It started in earnest on 12 March and by 14 March all of Scotland's pits were at a standstill . . .

They expected . . . the rest of the pits would follow Cortonwood, to support them, that's what they call the domino effect, but [while] a lot of them did, a lot of them didn't, and more so the Notts coalfield . . . their membership voted to stay in until such time as they got a national ballot, and that was refused!   *John Gillon, Clackmannan.*

There was no argument up here . . . in Scotland we were solid, we were not interested in a ballot.   *John McCormack, Polmaise.*

As union officials, we put a picket line on at Monktonhall and not a single man crossed it. Then I went to Newbattle workshops (where I was also delegate for the NUM men) and argued that they should come out on strike – which they did – and Bilston Glen also came out on strike, so it was rolling strike up here.   *David Hamilton MP, Midlothian.*

I worked as a canteen assistant in Killoch Colliery . . . it worried me going in through these picket lines . . . I tossed and turned on the Friday night and thought no, I'm not doing it . . .

'phoned the canteen manageress to say I would not be going to work on Monday . . . and she told me then that COSA (The Colliery Office Staff Association) had come out, but I had taken my decision prior to knowing about theirs, so I felt good about that.

Liz Marshall, Ayrshire.

The first day the strike happened . . . I saw all the pickets at the gate [of Bilston Glen] stood back and watched, and thought this is serious, but I wasn't union minded at the time so I went home. I stood on the picket line the next day and watched what was happening. No way I was crossing the picket line; there was my friends, people I work with, my brothers . . . I just gradually got more involved. *James Hogg, Midlothian.*

Once men are out on the cobblestones they've made the initial sacrifice, done away with three or four weeks' wages and are getting into the fight . . . it was ludicrous not to ballot because we would have won that ballot and the ball game would have been different.

David Hamilton MP, Midlothian.

We were fighting . . . to keep our jobs, we didn't want to lose the pit, it was the main employer in our area, if that pit closed what were we going to do?

James Hogg, Midlothian.

We were fighting for our communities, a way of life and the fabric of British society, because we were convinced that Thatcher was tearing it to bits.

Neil Valentine, Ayrshire.

When you're fighting for your pits and your communities you've got to do it whichever way is best and I didn't think we had any option. *Jim Tierney, Clackmannan.*

I think the strike was unavoidable.

Alex Bennett, Midlothian.

Kay McNamara

Scottish Mining Museum

COAL, THE NATION'S ENERGY FUTURE

SAVE IT WITH THE NUM

NO PIT CLOSURES

SAVE YOUR JOB!

Courtrooms and cash

The NUM's area HQ at 5 Hillside Crescent, Edinburgh, ran the strike in Scotland, and Scottish Area officers also looked after the national union's strike funds . . .

Under the rules in Scotland . . . it was legal for us to go to our branches and take a show of hands, come back and vote at a delegate conference. *David Hamilton MP, Midlothian.*

The Scottish Area was taken to the High Court in Edinburgh and our lawyers put the case that we did everything possible to get the feelings of the men without a ballot . . . and we won the case, so we became the financial treasurer of the strike funds. The strike was challenged in the English courts, on a financial basis, and the funds were sequestrated, which meant that Scotland had to act as the banker – if the national union wanted money we sent it to them – and got receipts! *Eric Clarke, Midlothian.*

During the strike the one area they couldn't touch was Scotland. They were sequestrating the NUM funds, except in Scotland, because the judges deemed that the Scottish area had acted within the rules of the union. *David Hamilton MP, Midlothian.*

I used to go down to the national executive, we paid their expenses and if we got two day's notice we took English money, and if we only got one day's notice we took Scottish. At one time I had £20,000 in a suitcase and I left in the morning, and took it down on the train – but every penny was accounted for! *Eric Clarke, Midlothian.*

A lot of folk were saying, in hindsight, we should have had a ballot, and maybe they were right . . . people in Nottingham and

In every mining village they look around for the most miserable character they can get and make him the treasurer – and I was the treasurer for Scotland, so you know what that makes me! *Eric Clarke, treasurer of the NUM's Scotland Area.*

Yorkshire had been brainwashed into thinking that if they got rid of the peripheral areas they would get a better coal industry and more money, and we were frightened of people having the right to vote us out of a job, and if they voted against the strike that was them voting for the closure of Scotland's collieries.

Eric Clarke, Midlothian.

We were fighting against the state . . . the stakes were so high, the government could not be seen to be defeated.

David Hamilton MP, Midlothian.

It cost this country millions, if not billions, of pounds to beat the miners and she [Mrs Thatcher] would have gone on and on and bankrupted the country, just to beat us.

Eric Clarke, Midlothian.

Stocking up at a strike centre.

Fife Mining Archives/John Beal

Strike centres set up

There were regional strike centres at Ayr, Cardowan, Dalkeith, Dysart, Fishcross and Whitburn, and these had a number of sub-centres attached to them.

Each community had its own strike centre and strike committee. They took information from the central office in Ayr about what areas had to be picketed . . . you put your name forward and they drew up a list. It was just like working in the pit!

Barney Menzies, Ayrshire.

Kay McNamara

Fife Mining Archives/John Beal

I, along with a fella called Pat Egan, set up the strike centres at Twechar, Kilsyth and Croy, the main one was Kilsyth, at the Bogside Hall – I went up to Kilsyth and Cumbernauld District Council to see about it and the boy says 'Och! this will be over in a week – stay there as long as you want, but it will be finished in a week.'   *Tom Canavan, Cardowan.*

We had 24 strike centres [in Ayrshire] . . . a lot of people felt isolated because of the circumstances and it was all about getting them together and getting them involved.

Bert Smith, Ayrshire.

We had about twenty strike centres in this area, centralised in the strike centre at Dalkeith.   *Alex Bennett, Midlothian.*

The men always had their meetings at Dalkeith . . . Loanhead had their own strike centre, as did Danderhall; Newtongrange had their own centre where they fed the people as well.   *Margo Russell, Midlothian.*

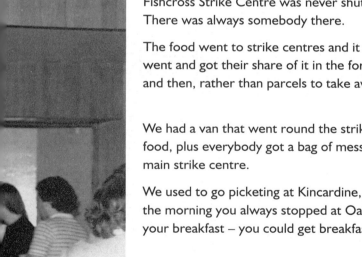

Fishcross Strike Centre was never shut, it was open 24 hours a day. There was always somebody there.   *William Muir, Clackmannan.*

The food went to strike centres and it was used collectively. People went and got their share of it in the form of food to eat right there and then, rather than parcels to take away with them.

Neil Valentine, Ayrshire.

We had a van that went round the strike centres and distributed food, plus everybody got a bag of messages every week from the main strike centre.   *Tom Canavan, Cardowan.*

We used to go picketing at Kincardine, and if you were out early in the morning you always stopped at Oakley on the way back to get your breakfast – you could get breakfast up to a certain time of day.

Andrew Stark, Fife.

Jimmy and Tam ran the strike centre in Oakley Welfare. They would be there with the breakfasts at 4 o'clock or 5 o'clock in the morning after we'd been somewhere like the Frances, then at 9 o'clock for everybody that was picketing locally. At 2 o'clock or 3 o'clock in the afternoon, dinner was there for everybody.   *Bobby Clelland, Fife.*

Women declare their support for the strike.

Women mobilise

As the strike deepened women started to get involved, setting up soup kitchens and generally providing support . . .

When the strike happened it was a case of everyone muck in . . . we were asked if we could open a soup kitchen, and we just took it from there . . . I cooked things that needed longer in the house and it was just a matter of heating it up. Every mining family involved in the strike got their dinner every day, Monday to Friday. *Margaret Wegg, Cardowan.*

I had a bit of a struggle to begin with . . . because at that time the men were doing everything and did not really want women involved . . . but it changed very quickly. Men going on pickets were starving when they came back, so they decided that the women could run the kitchen – very sexist – but they quickly became reliant on the work we were doing and realised that women had a part to play. By the end of May, beginning of June, the women were thoroughly ensconced in the strike centres. We started at nine in the morning and finished at nine at night, and there would be a rota of two women on kitchen duty in three hour blocks preparing meals, serving meals, tidying up and just making sure that if anybody was going out on the picket lines there would be sandwiches ready for them.

Liz Marshall, Ayrshire.

The men made the breakfast in the morning and then we were there in the afternoon so people got at least one good square meal a day, Monday to Friday. So they could have soup, and then a main course and maybe apple pie.

Margo Russell, Midlothian.

The Cowdenbeath women's committee consisted of miners' wives, but there were daughters and a couple of young, unemployed women and they played a tremendous role in the daily graft of providing for people. You would get either a main meal, or soup and pudding daily. It wasn't as busy at the weekends as through the week. The men didn't leave all the cooking and washing up to the women, they mucked in as well because frankly if they hadn't, they would have been told – that's just the nature of the community really.

Cath Cunningham, Fife.

There were local women's strike committees as well as the Lothian and Scottish women's strike committees. The Scottish organised throughout the whole country and arranged trips abroad. People in other countries gave us holidays or sent money and gifts over, which we distributed to the Lothian women's strike centre. They distributed it to the local strike centres and asked them what they needed – clothes, money or food?

Jean Hamilton, Midlothian.

We went on the demos – I remember coming back wet and cold from one in London. I was in my bed for four days after that!

Margaret Wegg, Cardowan.

We started to have meetings along with the men – it was important because we could see what they were up against and we felt part of a unit.

Margo Russell, Midlothian.

The women wanted to organise a fund-raising do in Cowdenbeath strike centre. One of them knew Christian, the singer, and the men's committee were saying 'you'll never do it, he'll never come, nobody will come to see him, it will be a disaster', however he did come and the concert was a great success – and that was a great thing at a local level that a celebrity would do something like that for nothing, and it vindicated the girls' enthusiasm.

Cath Cunningham, Fife.

Scottish Mining Museum

Raising funds

A huge effort was put into fund-raising because people needed to subsist. Women went around the bakers and asked for any bread that was left over and donations of all sorts. *Cath Cunningham, Fife.*

Women were out raising money, talking to local folk, running bingos, coffee mornings or afternoons, raffles all the time – just anything to raise money. *Liz Marshall, Ayrshire.*

Fund-raising was co-ordinated from Fishcross – they would call Kelty and say 'could you send 12 boys through to Glasgow' – one of the favourite places was Central Station. *Andrew Stark, Fife.*

I went to Liverpool for a week, everybody took their turn in going, we got a lot of money there. The support we got in this area – Kirkintilloch, Kilsyth, Cumbernauld, Stepps – was out of this world! We bought an old minibus and that did picketing. It ran about, picked people up and took them into Glasgow every Saturday. *Tom Canavan, Cardowan.*

We were asked to go up to Pollok, in Glasgow, and stand there with the cans, fund-raising. We got donations of about £200–£290 of a weekend. *Liz Marshall, Ayrshire.*

With the Kirkintilloch fund-raising caravan behind, Bill Ferns, treasurer of the local strike centre, receives a cheque from the Provost of Strathkelvin District.

Picture courtesy of the *Kirkintilloch Herald*

A lot of support came from the caravan at George Square. One day a lady and her daughter left a cheque for £300; on the Saturday her daughter and son came in and one left £30 and the other £40 . . . she came in again near to Christmas and said she had two bikes, so we handed them into an auction.   *Bill Ferns, Cardowan*.

It didn't matter where you went there was big support – our best collecting place was Yarrow's shipyard; we went there once a month and came back with close on two or three thousand pounds.   *John McCormack, Polmaise*.

We had miners based in Belfast all through the strike . . . fund-raising and raising political awareness. To see the humanitarian aid the folk there gave to other people, when they had so much strife, probably worse than we ever had . . . was unbelievable.
                                          Barney Menzies, Ayrshire.

We had the donations from Colonel Gaddafi, which of course was used as political capital – we were not supposed to take that you see. The idea was that we were supposed to keep a stiff upper lip and starve to death!   *Neil Valentine, Ayrshire*.

Fife Mining Archives/John Beal

Kay McNamara

Blister break on a sponsored walk from Burntisland to Dundee.

A break at Wallyford for sponsored walkers who trudged through the rain to raise £230.

Kay McNamara

A cold shift in the fund-raising shop.

Community support

Ordinary people in mining communities did what they could to support the striking miners . . .

It was a community effort, it wasn't just the miners, it was the community that was involved, there was no question about that.
Barney Menzies, Ayrshire.

The funding came from a lot of local suppliers and the likes of Steven's the bakers, the local butcher, they donated things every week. *Andrew Stark, Fife.*

In Kilsyth we had a different shop to go to every day, one day it was the bakers who gave us stuff for nothing, next day it was the fish shop, next day it was the butchers. One Indian shopkeeper gave us milk and rolls every day. *Tom Canavan, Cardowan.*

Local businesses were supporting us – Stewart's the fishmongers gave vouchers . . . we got vegetables from a local man. *Margo Russell, Midlothian.*

The regular daily shopping was mostly done locally, and the shopkeepers all supported that. *Liz Marshall, Ayrshire.*

The shopkeepers wanted to support the miners strike, but they knew that if they didn't help them at that time, then, when things got back to normal, people would remember that and maybe not go back to that shop. *Cath Cunningham, Fife.*

Walter Banks, the local butcher in Sauchie, was very supportive of us, providing meat for the soup pot.
William Muir, Clackmannan.

When Paul Weichec, the local butcher, found out my husband was on strike he filled a bag with meat for us every week,

Kay McNamara

Children join a march in support of the strike.
Fife Mining Archives/John Beal

and did the same for other mining families. *Kay McNamara, Midlothian.*

We lived a lot on sausages and spam. *Liz Marshall, Ayrshire.*

We would be standing with collecting cans outside supermarkets and people would come out and donate two or three tins. *Margaret Wegg, Cardowan.*

One old woman . . . was in every week with £1, £2 or £3, other folk gave in baking, scones, pancakes. *Liz Marshall, Ayrshire.*

Not everyone supported the aims of the strike, but they empathised with the hardship that families went through, so some donations came conditionally . . . to be used for children or women, or for food for families. *Cath Cunningham, Fife.*

Middle-class people that we would never have come in contact with – offered us their house for a weekend, gave us theatre tickets and sent things like toiletries into the strike centre. May Hogarth, a middle-class lady from Selkirk, invited us to her home for a meal, we met her and her family. She went on picket duty and they didn't know how to handle her because she was quite elderly then. She had great stamina, great guts and it was an inspiration to a lot of us that somebody like that, who didn't have a background in mining, was happy to support us, so she was brilliant. *Margo Russell, Midlothian.*

Support
from brothers and others

The STUC and Trades Councils were very helpful, but new industrial relations laws restricted the type of support that other unions could offer, although many assisted with donations of cash and kind . . .

SOGAT (the print union) were brilliant, they collected money off their workers and sent van loads of food, family-sized tins of soup and stew, and that went out to every strike centre plus everybody got a bag of messages every week out of that.

Margaret Wegg, Cardowan.

There was a Co-operative bakery in Kilsyth at the time – an uncle of mine was the manager – SOGAT gave us these tins of stew and we took them to Kilsyth, and they made them into steak pies for us. *Tom Canavan, Cardowan.*

I know that Rosyth Dockyard was particularly good, finance came in from there and the Fire Brigades Union. *Pat Rattray, Fife.*

There was a lot of disappointment with the steel workers . . . you would have thought miners would have got at least some support from them. *Alex Bennett, Midlothian.*

Ravenscraig steelworks not only continued, they broke production records, but I'm not blaming the steel workers . . . I blame the leadership of that union. I blame some of the leadership of the transport drivers union too . . . having said that both the seamen's union and the dockers were unstinting in their support, and the railwaymen were wonderful.

Neil Valentine, Ayrshire.

The train drivers union (ASLEF) said they would not move coal, so trucks were hired from Yuill & Dodds.

Alex Bennett, Midlothian.

**Moral and material support from
SOGAT was significant.**

Scottish Mining Museum

Scottish Mining Museum

An 80 year old woman went into a shop in Ballingry, bought a tin of soup, walked out and lamped it right through a Yuill & Dodds' lorry window!   *Andrew Stark, Fife.*

Other trade unions were always giving money . . . the EIS, people like that, the Leith Communist and Labour Party got together and had a collection on a Saturday, and gave us that money – they adopted us.   *Margo Russell, Midlothian.*

We got tremendous support from Dundee. We went up and spoke to other trade unionists and explained to them what the strike was about, and why it was important to support it, and people went back into heir workplaces and organised collections.
Cath Cunningham, Fife.

Unbeknown to us, nurses at the Edinburgh Royal Infirmary had a collection, and donated it to the Musselburgh strike centre.   *Kay McNamara, Midlothian.*

The council gave the striking miners free entry to the open air swimming pool at Cumnock, so we didn't have to pay for any facilities, tennis, putting greens, anything, so they did their best for us.
Barney Menzies, Ayrshire.

We had great support from Strathkelvin District Council, and Cumbernauld and Kilsyth District Council. We used to play one off against the other!   *Bill Ferns & Tom Canavan, Cardowan.*

When I went back to work I had a year's rent to pay Clackmannan Council, I think it was over two years, but I had to pay it back.   *William Muir, Clackmannan.*

Polkemmet was half in Lanarkshire and half in Lothian – Lanarkshire men were getting help from Strathclyde Region, but Lothian Region was under Tory control.
Alex Bennett, Midlothian.

ASLEF, the train drivers' union, joins a march in support of the miners.

Fife Mining Archives/John Beal

Strathclyde Regional Council wanted money given to striking miners or their families accounted for, and we had to give a pledge to pay all that back – on the basis of £1 or £2 a week.

Barney Menzies, Ayrshire.

It wasn't charity, you wouldn't have wanted that, it was a means of survival.

Liz Marshall, Ayrshire.

Kay McNamara

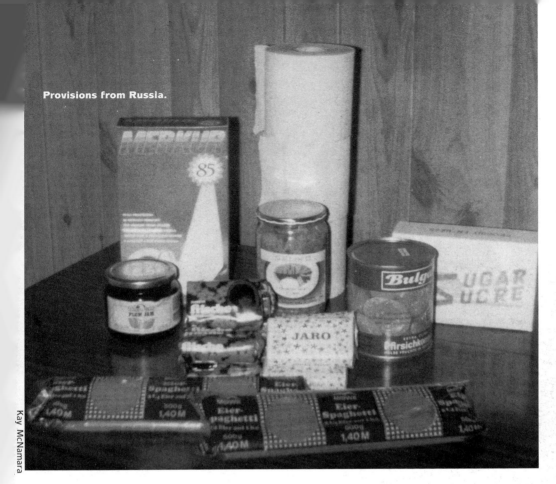

Provisions from Russia.

Kay McNamara

Carrots, peas and Serbian bean soup

Food parcels came from Russia – day to day things like sugar, it was different from the sugar we get. The toilet rolls were not the best quality!   *Andrew Stark, Fife.*

We went to the Co-operative in Edinburgh where this big articulated lorry was sitting . . . and all you could see was carrots and peas (together!) in glass jars, and Serbian Bean Soup . . . it took several vans to empty this lorry load back to Fishcross – the floor in the Miner's Welfare almost gave way. The carrots and peas were very good; the Serbian Bean Soup – it was an acquired taste!   *David Carruthers, Clackmannan.*

It was pretty awful!   *Neil Valentine, Ayrshire.*

My wife hated it!   *James Hogg, Midlothian.*

We got provisions sent from East German miners, and the Soviet Union sent what they could . . . strange cabbagy things that probably, nowadays – funny old world – you'd probably pay a fortune for in a delicatessen, but it was amazing how we could use these things. It maybe widened our horizons instead of eating Norrie's pies all the time!   *Cath Cunningham, Fife.*

THE MINER

SPECIAL ISSUE

JOURNAL OF THE NATIONAL UNION OF MINEWORKERS

FRIDAY 2 NOVEMBER 1984

Board in tatters as talks founder

INTERNATIONAL AID POURS IN

The French are here . . . and it's a glorious sight. Food and cash aid is now building up around the world, and these French miners chipped in with a mammoth collection of 400 tonnes of food back home. More pictures and report — Page 7.

The Coal Board's top leaders are in total disarray following collapse of the latest round of tal...

Sackings, gaggings re-instatements "enforced holidays" has placed the wh... NCB negotiating team at sixes a... sevens, making sensible talks impossi...

The Board simply broke off the negotiat... at ACAS, although the NUM made plain t... it was fully prepared to continue the talk...

Now a power struggle at the highest le... is on the cards, possibly leading to the ea... departure of Ian MacGregor.

At the talks, meaningful progress became an impossibility with the tattered Coal Board blindly following the so called NACODS formula, a form of words which in effect does nothing whatever to defend the mining industry.

The formula's essence is that intended closures, including those which sparked off the dispute, could be referred to a third party whose views would be taken into account by the board.

It still leaves the Coal Board free to ignore those views and close pits on any grounds it chooses.

Pits currently under threat would only be reconsidered in line with the procedure and the overall cutback strategy not withdrawn.

The Board would be able to carry out its closure programme unrestricted.

The position of the NUM — as put at earlier ACAS talks — remains wholly principled and clear.

● Withdrawal of the 4m tonnes cutback plan which because of changing circumstances is now obviously a nonsense.

● Withdrawal of the plan to shut five na... collieries, which for same reasons is also nonsense.

● No closures on eco... mic grounds, as the wh... basis for such closu... (see centre pages) is utt... ly false.

● A healthy, expandi... and sensibly run indus... in line with the Plan... Coal providing a secu... energy future for Brita...

Coming apart

The chances of getti... logical responses to the proposals were howev... made impossible by t... infighting at the Board... top levels and the obvio... interference at a politic... level.

With November no... here the outward appea... ance of Coal Board... Government calm is con... ing apart at the seam... internally with both lea... ing Board figures and i... dividual Ministers sayi... privately that the curren... position cannot be mai... tained much longer.

In the coming week... the rows are expected t... break into the public are... na more often.

The most likely cours... is that it will lead to Mac... Gregor's dismissal, a pub... lic clearing of the air and then progress will be made.

STOP PRESS

Secret Coal Board document exposed by NUM President showing almost total destruction of North East coalfield by turn of century with only four pits remaining. Similar cutbacks for Scotland revealed. Full list and details in next issue of *The Miner*.

Meanwhile NEC decides on recalled special delegates' conference for November 5th as new drive is mounted for greater support from movement in line with TUC conference decision. Government, on the other hand, trying to distance itself from Ian MacGregor as NCB "own goals" pile up. Pound coming under renewed pressure as strike forces Government to exceed borrowing targets by £1.5 billion.

got sent a small bag of corn; whoever was the propagandist through there must have told them that we were right in the grubber – there was a note inside it 'hoping you have a good harvest'. I got a suit from a bank manager in Holland, with a note in the pocket, so I knew where it came from, and corresponded with him for a number of years.

David Carruthers, Clackmannan.

Lorries arrived from Georgia, Russia . . . with plastic bags full of clothes . . . we packed a room at the Woodburn Community Centre to the ceiling and still had loads left so we went down to Musselburgh and jam packed a big room there. About 30 per cent of the stuff was quite reasonable – you had no money to buy clothes so you had no choice really.

James Hogg, Midlothian.

You felt ungrateful because these were workers in other countries, whose standard of living was probably ten times worse than ours, giving up something to send to us, so on the one hand it was really humbling . . . but on the other, for example, there were boots that were like pit boots and none of our kids would have worn them!

Cath Cunningham, Fife.

We got clothes from Norway . . . and we thought we could use this to our advantage, so we opened a wee shop . . . and took our turn in manning that as well . . . it gave us a chance to say to people we're not the ogres that Maggie is trying to make us out to be.

Margo Russell, Midlothian.

I was asked to go across to Germany to speak [after the strike] . . . I spent a month there. The money I collected was unbelievable . . . that was just Germany, the support we had must have been world wide.

Jim Tierney, Clackmannan.

Picketing

The strike centres directed pickets to wherever they were needed at collieries, docks or depots . . .

You've heard the quote about war, it was like that, a lot of boredom interspersed with periods of excitement – standing with maybe 5,000 people at your back, and a serried row of policemen at your front, and you're being pushed towards them, that's quite exciting!

Ian Robb, Cardowan.

There were times, when the adrenaline was running, it was really exciting. Sometimes when you were picketing, there was lots of pushing and shoving going on – when it stopped I could feel my body shaking!

Pat Rattray, Fife.

Ayrshire was well organised and we had an army . . . you name it and they were there . . . cannon fodder if you like!

Neil Valentine, Ayrshire.

We went to London to lobby parliament. *Andrew Stark, Fife.*

One of the first things we did was go over and picket Belfast docks because of all the coal ships that were coming in there. *Barney Menzies, Ayrshire.*

Coal was coming in (to Ireland) from Poland . . . hoardings advertising Polish coal sprang up all along the motorways and everywhere. It was bizarre! However, the strike was very active in Northern Ireland, Kilroot power station was wound down significantly.
Neil Valentine, Ayrshire.

We were through at Ravenscraig steelworks . . . they were importing foreign coal through Hunterston . . . so there was big picketing through there, and at Hunterston, but it made no difference. *Alex Bennett, Midlothian.*

We bought a van from the proceeds of a collection at a football match – I think it was the Scottish Cup Final. We covered Hunterston seven days a week, twelve months of the strike, every day, three shifts with this 'picket van' as they called it. *Bert Smith, Ayrshire.*

Scottish Mining Museum

Picketing – 'a lot of boredom interspersed with periods of excitement'. *Ian Robb, Cardowan.*

had a theory about police horses – read it somewhere, or heard it on the telly, maybe in a cowboy film – if you kneel down, the horse will instinctively jump over you, so I did that when the police charged us at Hunterston and the next thing I woke up with blood everywhere and my nose burst – so that was that theory out the window.

Bobby Clelland, Fife.

The women were not just happy to stay in the soup kitchen, if we had a bus going to Ayrshire, to Killoch etc., so many of them wanted to come, they were not afraid to get involved.

James Hogg, Midlothian.

An opencast on the road between Cardenden and Lochgelly was seen as a cushy picket because cars used to give a peep of encouragement or stop and give the pickets fags, juice, and pies, so everybody wanted to do that one!

Cath Cunningham, Fife.

A cold shift at Monktonhall.
Kay McNamara/Jim Angus

Miners run from a police charge.
Picture courtesy of John Sturrock/Network Photographers

Orgreave:
A defining moment

Arthur Scargill chose to mount a mass picket at Orgreave coke works in Yorkshire. The action began in late May and rose to a crescendo on 18 June when over 10,000 miners, many from Scotland, arrived for a final showdown.

It was a picket and it was violent.

Ian Robb, Cardowan.

People wanted to go down and show solidarity . . . at the same time they knew they were going to get a hammering . . . but the bus was full — there were people clambering to get on. After they went away the mood in the strike centre was very low.

Cath Cunningham, Fife.

We went down with a pack of sandwiches, a packet of crisps, and a wee bottle of juice.

'Spud' Porterfield, Fife.

Six bus loads went from Ayrshire and they were shown where to go; 'your bus is down this road here and the picketing is along there'.

Bert Smith, Ayrshire.

The police were so helpful getting us into Orgreave. They stopped the bus and we thought Oh! that's it, they're going to turn us about.   *Ian Robb, Cardowan.*

They said 'Just follow us': they were taking us right into it; we should have smelled a rat right there and then.   *Tom Canavan, Cardowan.*

There were police there who were not police, they had no uniform on . . . there were army there that day.   *Bill Ferns, Cardowan.*

There were thousands of police; we were getting lured into a war, it was like a battle. It was a blisteringly hot day, there were boys up the top sitting about in T-shirts or stripped to the waist, just sunning themselves . . . it was too quiet so the police sent the horses in, charged us, and smashed miners over the head with their truncheons when they retreated.   *Pat Rattray, Fife.*

I landed down the bottom of a bank . . . and when I came to I heard this snarl – the police had dogs on run-out leads there. *Pat Rattray, Fife*.

Picture courtesy of John Sturrock/Network Photographers

And Scargill shouted; 'we get this every day – back in again boys, have another go at them!'
                                                                    Tom Canavan, Cardowan.

The police gave no quarter, just got laid into them. A boy, who wasn't involved in the strike, came out of a house and a policeman came up behind and rattled him with his baton.
                                                                    Pat Rattray, Fife.

The police all had big batons and they chased us up through a housing scheme and through back gardens.
                                                                    'Spud' Porterfield, Fife.

A boy ran through a woman's house, out the back door and right through her greenhouse; right through the glass.
                                                                    David McArthur, Fife.

We had a couple of boys lifted . . . one got truncheoned stupid, he was on the national news getting taken away with blood streaming down his face.
                                                                    'Spud' Porterfield, Fife.

Wee Willie – he was five and a half stone and five foot two inches – got lifted and charged with police assault! At court he was told to stand up, he said 'I am standing'.
                                                                    Bill Ferns, Cardowan.

Of the 103 charged with violence that day, not one was ever found guilty because all the charges were dropped, there was no evidence against them. It was the BBC and STV people who showed all that violence on the television, who lied to the public, they showed you the miners throwing stones and the police reacting. It was the other way round, it was the police who charged into the miners . . . who just picked up bricks and retaliated.
                                                                    James Hogg, Midlothian.

They took a tanking that day and it made you reflect quite a lot about where we were going with this strike, and realise what we were up against in terms of the force, the resources and finance that the government was prepared to put in to ensure that the outcome would be in their favour.
                                                                    Cath Cunningham, Fife.

Police

At the beginning of the strike local police officers were on the picket line and the relationship was pretty good – a number of the police that were on the picket lines came from mining communities or mining backgrounds. That changed after a month or two, they started bringing in police from other regions, we had the Borders police up. Down south, the Metropolitan Police were ruthless . . . if you shouted at them the wrong way, you were arrested, if you looked at them the wrong way, you were arrested . . . everybody seemed to be six and a half feet, seven feet tall . . . they were vicious and they loved it – one policeman says 'I hope this strike continues' . . . because they were earning so much money.
                                                                    David Hamilton MP, Midlothian.

An arrest at Bilston Glen.
Picture courtesy of *The Scotsman:* www.scotsman.com

I gave a talk about the police and how they justified what they were doing. In it I used the example of a riot I'd seen at a football match where needless violence led to fifteen arrests, and contrasted that with a picket at New Cumnock where 87 men were herded into a field like animals, taken to Ayr police station and charged with contravention of the 1875 conspiracy act. *Liz Marshall, Ayrshire.*

It was unbelievable how they could thump miners for breach of the peace fines of £200 a time, first time offences. *Barney Menzies, Ayrshire.*

Boats were coming in to Perth with coal from Poland . . . it got a bit rough. On the way back I got to the end of the Inches and a policeman stopped me and said 'where are you going?' – I said 'home'. 'Where have you come from?' I said 'the docks', and he asked where did I get the car and was it paid for – he wouldn't let me pass – so I got out of the car, locked it, left it sitting in the middle of the road and sat on the grass – and stopped the traffic until he apologised and he's snarling through his teeth 'I'm sorry'.   *Pat Rattray, Fife.*

Pickets set off in six buses heading for Hunterston and were stopped by half of the Glasgow constabulary at Stepps.   *Tom Coulter, Clackmannan.*

I was in the first bus and this old geyser with the braid and that on his cap says to the bus driver 'turn back', and the driver says to me 'we've to turn back', so I goes out to him and says 'what's the problem?', and he says 'where are you going?', I says, 'we're going on a picnic' 'a picnic?', I says 'aye'. So we opened up the boot and there's all the pies and sandwiches, but before you could say Jake Robertson there was motors coming from everywhere, boom, boom across the road, and the men were saying 'what are we going to do?', and I says 'get out in the middle of the road they cannae the lift the lot of us' – and they lifted every one of us – 295 men!   *John McCormack, Polmaise.*

The miners' club phone was tapped, so the men used to say they were going to one place when in fact they were going somewhere else. So the police went to the wrong place.
                                    Margo Russell, Midlothian.

We tested suspicions of phone tapping one day at the Frances pit. There must have been

Incident at Stepps.

Sam Cowie

500 or 600 pickets and a lot more police, bussed in from Dundee. They were expecting big trouble, but we had set them up because when the scab buses went in we all walked off. A baffled policeman says 'you can't leave, I've got all these men here'.

Andrew Stark and Pat Rattray, Fife.

If you were active during the strike most of the local police got a bead on you . . . they would follow you, or stop you and say 'where are you going?'   *Pat Rattray, Fife.*

There were two guys in a car at Mayfield roundabout . . . in plain clothes, sitting in a plain car, checking on the pickets . . . you were always getting watched, and they were always trying to get you to 'grass' . . . windows getting smashed and they were trying to find out who it was.

James Hogg, Midlothian.

That year demonstrated to anyone who wants to look at it that the police force is a political weapon and will do the bidding of their political masters, and will break and ignore the law of the land when it suits them. I'd never trust them; I'd rather trust a tramp in the street than a police officer.

Neil Valentine, Ayrshire.

Incident at Stepps.
Sam Cowie

Drawing by Jim Douglas

Not everything went according to plan

The comical thing about Perth . . . everybody was busy watching a boat because a woman came off it with practically nothing on. We were all staring at this — next thing we heard engines started and the lorries were fleeing out the dock and we're all still looking at the bird!

Pat Rattray, Fife.

There was a picket at Kilmarnock Power Station — the police had batons and wee shields. They started coming towards us hitting their shields; thump, thump, thump — it was quite ominous, this big body of policemen intent on driving through us, but our line just opened up and they just went past and the boys were all clapping 'Oh! the grand old Duke of York'. It was priceless!

Neil Valentine, Ayrshire.

Some of the women occasionally got together on Friday nights . . . we would each buy a bottle of the cheapest plonk and it all went into a pot — that was 'picket's punch' — and we had a bloody good night!

Liz Marshall, Ayrshire.

The strike centres bartered with each other — Kelty had mince and Oakley had chickens, but when we went through with the mince we found that the chickens were still alive, and we had to catch them first!

Andrew Stark, Fife.

We had a big skip outside one of the shops that was derelict and people were going shopping and putting tins in — as a collection for the striking miners — and a couple of old women who went past didn't get the point, and took tins out.

Cath Cunningham, Fife.

We had a boy who packed a suitcase and went away for three months during the strike and these guys, I think in Great Yarmouth, grabbed him and locked him in a cupboard. 'Do you know this man?', 'aye we know him', 'what strike centres are attached to Kelty and what's the area strike centre?', 'Fishcross, why, what's happening?', and they reply 'we've got hold of this boy, he's been around about everywhere, we thought he was a police spy'!   *Andrew Stark and Pat Rattray, Fife.*

Two policemen were sitting in their jeep one day at Solsgirth, blocking the gate. We crowded round it and were chatting, and they asked how we were doing, and how many were coming today, and while we were doing that the boys at the back were letting the air out of the tyres, so the cops had to push the jeep down the road.   *Bobby Clelland, Fife.*

We were coming back [from Killoch] . . . and the accelerator cable on the bus broke. We were stuck in the middle of nowhere, so I took the laces out of my boots, opened up the panel next to the driver's seat and tied my bootlace round the accelerator. I lay on my belly and the driver says 'right Jimmy' and I pulled on the lace – and did that 'till we got to Mayfield and then somebody took over from me, but I don't know what the driver did when the last person got off!   *James Hogg, Midlothian.*

When the first scab went back, a lot of the boys from New Cumnock picketed his house. The police arrived and whipped them all away [including] one man wearing a pair of slippers – he had only gone down the street for milk and stopped to see what was going on. He says, 'If this is what you get, going for a pint of milk, I'm taking my tea black from now on'!   *Neil Valentine, Ayrshire.*

Drawing by Jim Douglas

Drawing by Jim Douglas

Drawing by Jim Douglas

We had pickets at Rothesay Dock (Clydebank) every day and they soon discovered there were tunnels going under the Clyde. They housed electric cables, most were dead, so the guys were salvaging copper, but on one occasion they picked a live one and sawed through it – I wasn't there at the time, but heard the story. The lid flew off the manhole, there was a big cloud of smoke and this guy appeared up like a genie on skates. I don't know how he wasn't killed; his hand was severely injured and next thing they were rushing back to Glasgow in a car with his hand sticking out the window to keep it cool.

Ian Robb, Cardowan.

We were fortunate at Dalkeith because Clara, who worked at the canteen at Monktonhall, took charge of the kitchen. She was making a curry and an individual, who shall remain nameless, likes her curry quite hot and a relative of hers, who also likes her curry quite hot, were going in and out of the kitchen, tasting and putting their own curry sauce in, so in the end it was inedible – too many cooks basically – so Clara banned them from the kitchen for a while.

Margo Russell, Midlothian.

We were at Hunterston, and it was a particularly bad and violent day, really, really violent and after it was all finished – it was a beautiful summer's day – and me and Willie were still sitting on the hillside, and all the men had drifted away. There was thousands of police there and twelve police horses all in a row facing up this hill when a drunk boy comes over the top of the hill . . . and he stands in front of this sergeant's horse, a great big horse, and he's like this, 'you, you bastard' – and he practically had his finger up the horse's nostril – 'you are one ugly, dirty bastard, and that thing below you is not much better'.

Sam Cowie, Clackmannan.

Kay McNamara

Kay McNamara

The Polmaise banner held high at a rally in Glasgow's George Square.

Marches and

Glasgow.

Fife Mining Archives/John Beal

Fife Mining Archives/John Beal

demonstrations

Edinburgh.

London.

Fife Mining Archives/John Beal

Fife Mining Archives/John Beal

Lothian's Miners
RALLY

SATURDAY 25th AUGUST, 1984

Arthur Scargill
President N.U.M.

Ella Egan
Womans' Support

Hugh Ormiston
Industrial Chaplain

Alex Eadie
M.P. for Midlothian

ASSEMBLE 11.00am, KING'S PARK, DALKEITH
marching to COWDEN PARK, DALKEITH.
In the event of bad weather, march will terminate at
Woodburn Miners' Club.

Printed by RITCHIE of INVERESK, Musselburgh.

Kay McNamara

The long hot summer

A cold, wet summer might have helped the miner's cause, but the sun shone . . .

It was a great summer that year, like the tropics.   *Barney Menzies, Ayrshire.*

A lot of people said it was the best summer they ever had, because it was roasting hot. We organised trips, picnics and activities for kids; it didn't have to be anywhere spectacular, some folk got to Butlin's – other families went to East Germany on holidays given by the workers over there. It was decided at local level who went, names in a hat, that kind of thing.
Cath Cunningham, Fife.

Sunshine rally:
Arthur Scargill speaking at Dalkeith.

Some women and their children went to East Germany in the summer of 1984. They put us up in this lovely, brand new hotel for three weeks; fed us, clothed us, gave us money to spend – they opened a shop specially for us . . . and we'd all this money to spend in two hours – a substantial amount – and we were to buy what we liked – we couldn't spend it!
Jean Hamilton, Midlothian.

A visit to Butlin's.

I think about twenty kids from Netherthird strike centre went on holiday to Ireland; my two went twice, I think they were away for a week at Easter and two weeks in the summer – had a wonderful time,. Two men, Rusty and Guy, went camping up Loch Doon and took two or three of the young boys with them, and I suspect the boys just ran wild; my son thoroughly enjoyed it.   *Liz Marshall, Ayrshire.*

In the summer we bought a tent and took the kids away down to North Berwick, to Gullane for the day, and they had their meals down there.
Margo Russell, Midlothian.

The Dalkeith banner in Dalkeith, on the march to the rally at Cowden Park on 25 August.

Fife Mining Archives/John Beal

We did a couple of outings to Girvan and we all went down to the beach at Irvine. The club always did a yearly trip to Butlin's anyway, so the kids got there too.

Liz Marshall, Ayrshire.

Children on a summer outing.

Fife Mining Archives/John Beal

The shop steward at Larkfield Garage (Glasgow) supplied buses and they took us to Ayr, in fact we were going to Butlin's so often, it felt like every week.

Tom Canavan, Cardowan.

Kids came on demonstrations, and to them it would appear like a day out because you would all go together in the bus and have your sandwiches all made up. They would go for the walk on the demonstration which would culminate in a town square or park, and there was always nice things to do in the park.   *Cath Cunningham, Fife.*

The personal struggle

As the strike dragged on past the summer, people began to feel the strain and the bills mounted up . . .

When you think about what men did, to give up wages for a year, was phenomenal; it just shows you the lengths men can go to . . . how some of these guys who had mortgages could have been on strike for a year, it beats me, absolutely beats me how they could have managed it.

Jim Tierney, Clackmannan.

THE NATIONAL UNION OF MINEWORKERS
(SCOTTISH AREA)

....19......

District ....

Branch ....

From ....

I cannot speak as the wife of a striking miner, but, according to the D.H.S.S. I can speak as a striking miner as this is how they classify me. I am entitled as such. I am not eligible for any benefits. I have to keep my 2 children on family allowance + F.I.S. This makes me very bitter + angry, because I could choose not to work + be kept by the state.
At the start of the strike I was not sure about the role I could play, so stay with. But at the now I see that

Draft for a speech.

The sacrifice wasn't fair – individually – some people lost their homes, their families, their life because of the worry.

Eric Clarke, Midlothian.

I got a 'phone call from a woman about one boy . . . he was totally destitute . . . I went to see him and all he had left in his house was a table and a telly, he'd got rid of everything, just to survive . . . we supplied him with food, toothpaste, soap, things like that . . . the DSS thought he was a genuine case and he got something like £10, but that was later changed and because he was on strike he got nothing – that was the policy then, because he was single.

Alex Bennett, Midlothian.

As a single man at the time I got next to nothing, so we went picketing, that's where we got our money – I think it was £1.

Barney Menzies, Ayrshire.

I think picket pay was something like £2 a stint for eight hours.

Bert Smith, Ayrshire.

Pickets were entitled to £2 or £3 a day – it was a struggle all right.

Bill Ferns, Cardowan.

We got the opportunity at Cumnock Juniors social club – where the Cumnock strike centre was – to do the bouncing at the local dances, so that was their way of giving us a wee bit of extra money.

Barney Menzies, Ayrshire.

I wrote to the mortgage companies and they were sympathetic – as long as the striking miners realised they would have to pay extra when the strike was over . . . it was the same with the Gas Board . . . they could have turned the gas off, but they didn't as long as people understood they had to pay it back.

Alex Bennett, Midlothian.

As a 'striking miner' with two children I got £17.95 per week in child benefit. You had to have proof that you were on benefit to get the clothing grant for the kids going back to

Liz Marshall

Children in an Ayrshire mining community.

school . . . you got no benefits if you had no proof, but the social work department stamped it and that allowed us to get the clothing grant, and they also got us money for shoes; it was money to use in other ways you saw fit.   *Liz Marshall, Ayrshire.*

A lot of the kids got their meals at school, because they would be entitled to free meals, but because of the way the benefits agency were handling it – the argument was that people were getting money from the union, and of course they weren't.

Margo Russell, Midlothian.

We had a year-long strike and I saw grown men cry during that year because of their debts and their worries . . . people did have it difficult, it broke families, it broke marriages, things like that.   *Andrew Stark, Fife.*

I'd just bought a car . . . was doing my house up . . . got letters from the bank . . . eventually the final demands were coming in . . . I just stuck it out; lost the house in December, my wife was devastated – we had put in a lot of time and effort to the house – it was an emotional time.   *James Hogg, Midlothian.*

The mortgage side of things must have been frightening . . . and hire purchase firms were not the most sympathetic. People tried to make sure the kids had enough, rather than

Fife Mining Archives/John Beal

Children proudly wear the badge of their dads' involvement in the strike.

Fife Mining Archives/John Beal

'Minors supporting miners'.

themselves, the priority was to make sure that everybody went out with clean clothes on.

Margo Russell, Midlothian.

The strike committee had to make sure that people had advice about benefits because the government changed the rules in that you could normally claim for everybody in the family, but because the miners were striking voluntarily . . . there was less money coming in than if you were on income support – it was a punitive measure to warn people that they could not just go off on strike, and that if they did they were going to suffer.

Cath Cunningham, Fife.

It was a problem in the winter, with heating. The new city by-pass was being built at Gilmerton. There was an outcrop of coal there and the miners went during the night and filled bags of coal and did the same on the stretch of the A1 between Prestonpans and Wallyford. We had squads logging and cutting up old railway sleepers and bagging them.

Alex Bennett, Midlothian.

There's a lot of families out there with men who stayed out for the full year who would have been forced back. I'm quite sure the strike would have been broken much sooner if their parents and extended family hadn't supported them.

Liz Marshall, Ayrshire.

There were five of us all together living in my mother's house, all on strike – she was 100 per cent behind us, believed in what we were doing . . . she couldn't do enough for us.   *James Hogg, Midlothian.*

My husband and I got married during the strike . . . local shops supplied cold meat and that sort of thing, and the club announced that if anybody wanted to come they were welcome. It was a great night, so we've got good memories of that and our marriage certificate says 'Married in Dalkeith Miners Club'.

Margo Russell, Midlothian.

I think there was a lot of pressure from families to go back to work, especially after the summer when it was looming towards Christmas.   *Alex Bennett, Midlothian.*

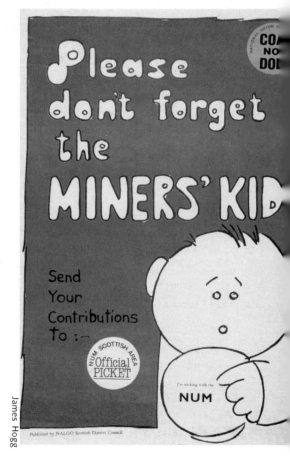

James Hogg

Please don't forget the MINERS' KIDS

CO NO DOL

Send Your Contributions to :–

SCOTTISH AREA NUM Official PICKET

I'm sticking with the NUM

Published by NALGO Scottish District Council

Kay McNamara

Cutting logs for pensioners.

Christmas 1984

It was the best and worst Christmas: it was the worst build-up to Christmas because people were so worried . . . however, material things aside, it was the best Christmas for a lot of families because of all the activity that went on, there were parties – we were up late nights wrapping presents for kids – we got really unusual toys from East Germany . . . and when kids opened it, it was 'Oh! this is unusual I bet none of my pals have got this'.

Cath Cunningham, Fife.

We got a lot of toys from France just before Christmas, French dolls, things like that, they were all part of what we handed out to the kids.   *Margo Russell, Midlothian.*

We got a delivery of toys from the Glasgow Trades Council. We had to parcel them up in the school and every kiddie got a toy – every strike centre got so many and they distributed them out.   *Margaret Wegg, Cardowan.*

Kay McNamara

Christmas card based on the strike message.

We went to negotiate the best deal for vouchers for Christmas, and my sister in law Nancy had £50,000 under her mattress before we took this bag of money to different stores to see if they would give us a special discount, and the only one that would entertain us was British Home Stores in Princes Street.

Jean Hamilton, Midlothian.

We decided to have a Christmas draw for a miners' lamp – we bought them off the Coal Board for £30 . . . and two or three of us went out and chapped doors and raised £300 so it wasn't a bad night's work, and that was to pay for the bairns' Christmas party.   *Alex Bennett, Midlothian.*

We also went to the Kelvin Hall Carnival.
Tom Canavan, Cardowan.

At Christmas, everybody – every family – got a hamper and there was a big turkey in every hamper – Cardowan Strike Centre did a deal with Farmfoods – that's where they came from – absolutely delicious – brilliant.   *Bill Ferns, Cardowan.*

I was involved in Northern Ireland with the raising of money to buy a turkey – a 25 pound turkey for every strike centre in Ayrshire – and an individual chicken for every household with a striking miner!

Barney Menzies, Ayrshire.

We all got chickens at Christmas from Chunky Chickens.   *Cath Cunningham, Fife.*

We were given turkeys by someone in Dalkeith, so we made sure that everyone got one who was on our list . . . we had a Christmas party for the kids and they had the panto in Edinburgh – the Lothian Women's Support Group negotiated for the tickets.   *Margo Russell, Midlothian.*

Donations of presents.

Kay McNamara

Christmas at the strike centre.

A MESSAGE TO SCOTTISH MINERS

All over Britain miners are returning to work.

Now is the time to get back to your pit.

If you return on or before November 19th you can look forward to earning up to £1400 before Christmas.

Your jobs will be protected by the National Coal Board.

If you want to return to work contact your colliery manager. He is ready to make the transport arrangements to get you back to work.

NCB
SCOTLAND

The NCB published advertisements designed to entice men back to work . . .

. . . and the NUM responded with a campaign of their own.

Drift-back

The trickle of men drifting back to work grew as the strike stretched unendingly into 1985 . . .

The Coal Board were trying this campaign . . . in the summer of '84 to break the strike, but by then I was 100 per cent behind the strike . . . there was no way I was going back.   *James Hogg, Midlothian.*

The Edinburgh trades fortnight was the first in Britain to go on holiday, so the NCB put all of its efforts into breaking Bilston Glen . . . to try and break the national strike. They took out full page newspaper adverts saying if you come back for the one day you'll get four weeks wages – which was right because you would have your holiday pay – so there was a bribe taking place all the way through.
                David Hamilton MP, Midlothian.

THE MINING CRISIS – THE FACTS

WORK SECURITY AND A FUTURE

WHY HAS THE MINERS STRIKE LASTED NINE MONTHS

THE MINERS HAVE NO DEMANDS ON THE COAL BOARD. IT IS THE BOARD THAT INSISTS ON THE RIGHT TO CLOSE PITS WITHOUT ANY AGREEMENT WITH THE MINERS. NO UNION OR GROUP OF WORKERS COULD AGREE TO THIS.

Ian MacGregor (appointed without a ballot vote) declared in March that 20 pits must close and 20,000 jobs would go. This included Polmaise and Bogside in Scotland, resulting in the devastation of these close knit communities - and only a prelude to the destruction of the coal mining industry in Scotland.

Remember when mining jobs are lost, other workers jobs will go also - including steel, transport, manufacturing and other related industries.

The miners call on the Board to stand by the <u>existing signed agreement</u> between the Government, the Coal Board and the Unions, namely the 'Plan for Coal', which means an expanding industry and jobs for miners and others.

A miners victory is a victory for the Scottish people.

Miners thank the Scottish people for their support and ask them to keep it up.

All donations to: **MINERS RELIEF FUND**   5 HILLSIDE CRESCENT, EDINBURGH.

Protest outside Seafield Colliery as the bus carrying 'drift-backs' arrives.
Picture courtesy of Fife Council Museums – Kirkcaldy Museum and Art Gallery

Folk were encouraged to go back to get their redundancy, which was big, big money at the time. *Barney Menzies, Ayrshire.*

If you accepted redundancy you got £1,000 for every year you worked in the industry. Men could get lump sums over £30,000 – you could never save that in a lifetime, so there's no doubt that was a big influence. *Alex Bennett, Midlothian.*

The first people to take their redundancy money, to get out, were the guys who broke the strike, they were never interested in fighting for their community.
James Hogg, Midlothian.

It was a bad strike in many ways; it broke good men and it was sad watching them going back to work. *David Hamilton MP, Midlothian.*

When the first scabs went back in Oakley, we didn't just picket the pit, we picketed their houses as well. *Bobby Clelland, Fife.*

An unmistakable message for some 'drift-backs'.

Fife Mining Archives/John Beal

Pickets attempt to change the minds of 'drift-backs' at Bilston Glen.

Scottish Mining Museum

The scab buses had mesh on them, so the boys used to get eggs, blow them, put oil in them, and break them against the windscreen so, when they wiped the windscreen, the oil was smeared all over it.
Andrew Stark, Fife.

On the national media it was all 'anti' stuff they were putting out. It wasn't a balanced picture. After January the media was in its full glory, announcing how many people were back at their work.
Bert Smith, Ayrshire.

Somebody said to me that . . . there was a time after Christmas when people were not drifting back to work, they were haemorrhaging back.
Cath Cunningham, Fife.

The after Christmas folk don't have the same stigma attached to them . . . because folk were on their knees, there's no two ways about it.
Liz Marshall, Ayrshire.

It's maybe a difficult thing to say, but if you've been on strike from March through winter to say January, and you go back to work and are called a scab, that's hard.
Jim Tierney, Clackmannan.

There were different categories of scabs . . . super scabs were the ones who were organising people to go back to work and were quite blatant and aggressive about it . . . wagging their pay packet in front of the people who were out on strike.
Cath Cunningham, Fife.

The more men that went back the harder it was for those who were still out on strike – its easier to be on strike with solidarity than it is with a divided community.
David Hamilton MP, Midlothian.

I think men got disillusioned as the strike dragged on – it was a long time to be on strike and there was no light at the end of the tunnel.
Alex Bennett, Midlothian.

At the start of the strike you were stopping coal coming in . . . at the end of the strike you were stopping miners going back.
David McArthur, Fife.

Kay McNamara

National Coal Board
Hobart House, Grosvenor Place, London SW1X 7AE

CHAIRMAN   March 1985
Ian MacGregor

Dear Colleague,

This long strike is over. It has been severely damaging to the relationships between all of us who work in the industry. Workers have not just been in dispute with management; miners have been set against fellow miners, causing terrible strain to individuals, families and communities.

The strike has cost individual workers thousands of pounds in lost wages and the Board many millions of pounds in lost and damaged equipment. We have lost many coalfaces.

This strike was not of management's choosing nor of our making. Now that it is over, every effort must be made to restore harmony within the industry so that we can all resume our respective responsibilities to ourselves, our families, our communities and the industry that sustains us.

When normal working has been restored, management will discuss and settle important issues with your representatives, including your pay now and for the future.

Your colliery manager's first priority is the restoration of safe working. I am asking you for your personal co-operation in ensuring the safety of your fellow workers.

Sincerely,

Ian MacGregor

Liz Marshall

Miners returning to work with their banner held high.
Kay McNamara

The end of the strike

By the end of February 1985 over 50 per cent of the miners had gone back to work. The union ended the strike on 5 March, with an organised return to work . . .

OK it was an organised return to work, but it was still a defeat; you could parcel it up any way you want, but it was a defeat, and people were totally crushed by it. The women's committee went to the gate of Seafield . . . the men came round the corner in the bus and their body language was just as if they had been burst and every bit of life had been squeezed out of them. It was heartbreaking to see that, and when they saw our banner everybody was up at the windows banging on them I think they really appreciated the fact that we were there to encourage them. *Cath Cunningham, Fife.*

The Union called on us to go back on the Tuesday, not the Monday, and that's why the men who stuck out the strike were referred to as the 'Tuesday boys'.

Barney Menzies, Ayrshire.

All the miners that went back on the Tuesday got a wee silver badge. My proud boast is that I'm the only woman that I know of in Scotland that stayed out the whole time of the strike. I have my 'Tuesday girl' badge.   *Liz Marshall, Ayrshire.*

Nearing the end of the strike we felt we had to do something for the people (members of the public) who had been really good to us . . . so we presented them with miners lamps.
                                                                                                Bill Ferns, Cardowan.

Going back was difficult . . . despite letters welcoming me back from Mr MacGregor, management made it difficult.   *Liz Marshall, Ayrshire.*

There was an atmosphere between people who went back to their work prior to Christmas and those who went back after Christmas . . . and then there was the other atmosphere between both groups and the people who went back after the strike ended. Management knew it was a disjointed workforce and really put the boot into people.
                                                                                          Barney Menzies, Ayrshire.

After the strike men could not get out quick enough, they were totally sickened; sickened!
                                                                                          Alex Bennett, Midlothian.

As a canteen worker . . . I would get no big redundancy. So I needed a job and, for me, it was always about a job.   *Liz Marshall, Ayrshire.*

If we are a democratic union, which we are, then our membership should have got the right to a ballot . . . that's under the rule, we didn't get that right and I think that's where it fell.   *John Gillon, Clackmannan.*

The tactics were wrong, we were on strike for a year, employed every tactic under the sun, but I have still to be told how we could have overcome it, because they had effectively manoeuvred us into a corner where we could not get out.
                                                                                    David Hamilton MP, Midlothian.

I support the
VICTIMISED MINERS

Kay McNamara

Sacked

A white line painted at the colliery gate delineated Coal Board property; strikers crossing it could be sacked for trespass . . .

A scuffle broke out, a lot of the pickets charged and the police just grabbed anybody, and they grabbed my brother Michael, so he was the first one arrested at Bilston Glen.   *James Hogg, Midlothian.*

Bert Smith went on the bus taking the first man back to Killoch, to speak to him, but there were pickets at the gate and the bus wouldn't stop . . . and Bert got sacked for trespassing.

Barney Menzies, Ayrshire.

Kay McNamara

FULL AMNESTY FOR Sacked Miners

Sacked miners on holiday in Moscow, in 1987.
Tom Coulter and David Hamilton

Fife Mining Archives/John Beal

A float leads a march in support of the sacked miners.

Fife Mining Archives/John Beal

Marching in support of the sacked miners.

At the end there were 1,000 men sacked, 206 in Scotland: 46 came from Monktonhall, more than any other pit in Britain, 36 were sacked at Bilston Glen and 5 at Newbattle Workshops, so of the 206 most came from this area . . . because this was the place where the strike had to be broken.   *David Hamilton MP, Midlothian.*

We had quite a lot of men sacked and half of the branch didn't want to go back to work until those men had been reinstated, but the sacked men felt they would have a better chance of getting their jobs back if the men went back to work, but they never got their jobs back.   *John McCormack, Polmaise.*

I had a hard job getting work after the strike. Then the bloke I'm working for now got a contract at Rosyth dockyard. He submitted everybody's name and they were all accepted except me. I wrote to my MP . . . and magically got clearance, but they hotly denied there was any such thing as a blacklist.   *Sam Cowie, Clackmannan.*

After the strike a lot of the women went back to the kitchen sink, but Mary and myself kept going, trying to raise funds for the victimised miners at the STUC Conference, Labour Party – anybody that would give us a stall at their conference. We sold mining memorabilia: brass plaques, lamps, key rings, badges, painted plates, anything related to the mining industry. The banner was always round our table and we got great support.
                    Margaret Wegg, Cardowan.

We had a collection every week without fail at Castlehill for the sacked miners, that went on for a long time.
                    John Gillon, Clackmannan.

Our comrades back at work turned down a ballot for 50p per man to assist the victimised miners . . . I don't know what the percentage was, but it was high!
                    David Carruthers, Clackmannan.

The sacked miners were taken to Russia . . . families went to Georgia and we stayed in Moscow. We were there for three weeks, and it was Russian miners who gave up their holiday to give it to us.
                    James Hogg, Midlothian.

SCOTTISH MINERS RELIEF FUND

HIBS/HEARTS SELECT
–v–
SCOTTISH MINERS JUNIOR SELECT

MEADOWBANK STADIUM EDINBURGH

SUNDAY 1st DECEMBER 1985
KICK OFF 2pm

STAND TICKETS ONLY – £1

Kay McNamara

Demolition of Monktonhall Colliery.

After the strike

The Industry

Scotland's pits did not survive long – most had closed by the end of the 1980s. The NCB was renamed British Coal in 1987, and the industry was privatised in 1994. The one remaining Scottish mine was closed in 2002.

Pit closures:
1985 Polkemmet.
1985 Frances (mothballed).
1986 Comrie.
1986 Killoch.
1987 Polmaise.
1988 Seafield.
1989 Barony.
1989 Bilston Glen.
1989 Monktonhall (mothballed).

And an opening: Castlebridge Shaft, 1986, but the Longannet complex (of which it was part) closed in 2002.

What Scargill told us at the start was proven right; they cleared all the pits a few years after the strike with thousands and thousands of jobs going – one pit after another, like a domino effect, like he said, they're all closed. *James Hogg, Midlothian.*

The only thing we've got is opencasts, and lorries and trains loaded with coal leaving every day, and yet, no work for the young people.   *Bert Smith, Ayrshire*.

When I went into the pit the tradesmen took you under their wing and told you the right and wrong ways to do things; they took time to help you – that doesn't happen in industry now.

Andrew Stark, Fife.

Michael Heseltine told Eric Clarke in the House of Commons . . . that they were having to shut pits that were making a profit because nobody wanted the coal – there's over 100 opencasts in Scotland now, so where are they getting rid of the coal? There's more coal being produced in Ayrshire now than there was when Barony and Killoch were there.   *Bert Smith, Ayrshire*.

I think that even though it's a dirty industry, we should have kept the mines open so that we could develop clean coal technology – the mines are closed in Scotland, where's all the experience? What happens in twenty to thirty years time when they want to start mining coal again – and I think at some time or other they will – it's going to cost more money and maybe even lives because we're losing the experience. Look at where they're buying coal now – Colombia where they use eight year old kids, so of course it's going to be cheaper. Poland and Russia – what wages do they pay? Australia – how can it be cheaper unless it's subsidised? You cannot compete against that – we've got to abide by laws, and health and safety regulations that other countries don't have.

Andrew Stark, Fife.

A little Ayrshire girl shows allegiance to Arthur Scargill.

The biggest area of untapped coal in Britain, if not in western Europe, is at Canonbie, and they haven't touched it yet . . . but sooner or later they'll have to go for it, because they still cannot do without coal.   *Neil Valentine, Ayrshire*.

Scottish Mining Museum

Liz Marshall

After the strike

The People

Thatcher won, but the fabric of this society was shredded, torn up and destroyed.

Neil Valentine, Ayrshire.

The pit wasn't ideal, but it was a job that all the young boys could go to . . . now you see them just lying about.

Bert Smith, Ayrshire.

We have a generation of weans who have never seen their parents working and we have all the ills of society – they were not here twenty years ago.

Liz Marshall, Ayrshire.

We've lost a lot through it, the government knew quite well what would happen, it's almost as if they have rubbed out a whole way of life.

Cath Cunningham, Fife.

Check around the country you'll find closed miners' welfares, football teams, pipe bands, youth clubs – clubs of all kinds – all destroyed.

John McCormack, Polmaise.

It used to be that if you walked down the road it was hello!, hello!, hello! Now you could walk down the whole road and you'd never see one person or two people that you know – it's not the same – the community has gone.

Margaret Wegg, Cardowan.

In some ways the year after the strike was harder. It was a national strike, so hire purchase or mortgage payments could often be deferred, as long as you paid something – mind you we got a television repossessed by the Co-op! – but as soon as you went back to work, everybody wanted a piece of your wages.

Cath Cunningham, Fife.

Kelty is a growing commuter town now; we're twenty minutes from Edinburgh, twenty minutes from Perth the other way – there's no industry, no pits, no mill, even the Co-op is away – and that was a big thing in mining villages. I think the strike changed us; we're more politically minded now.

Pat Rattray, Fife.

It was a life-changing experience for me; I take a lot more interest in what goes on locally, in the community and that came from just being involved in the miners' strike; that changed me completely. Also, I'm the councillor for the area I live in now.

Barney Menzies, Ayrshire.

It was a big catalyst for a lot of women . . . it changed women's lives . . . with some it only changed their lives for that year and once the strike was over they went back to a traditional role, but with a lot of women, myself included, it was . . . 'I can do more than peeling tatties in a kitchen' . . . so it was life-changing for me.

Liz Marshall, Ayrshire.

I learned a lot, it helped make my character, mould me into the person that I am – I would not sell anybody down the river in adversity and would stick by them, that's what its done for me. I would do it all again, without hesitation.   *James Hogg, Midlothian.*

It was worth it in the sense that we went out and fought for something we believed in.
                                                                Andrew Stark, Fife.

I don't know if it was worth it, because we lost. Would I do it again? Aye I would do it again. Would I do it differently? I would certainly do it differently.   *Bobby Clelland, Fife.*

I would go through it again, I would say it was the best year of my life – there was some heartache in it, but looking back it was one of the best years of my life.   *Pat Rattray, Fife.*

It was unforgettable, basically.   *Ian Robb, Cardowan.*

I would not have missed it for anything.   *Sam Cowie, Clackmannan.*

I was proud to have been part of it.   *Kay McNamara, Midlothian.*

James Hogg

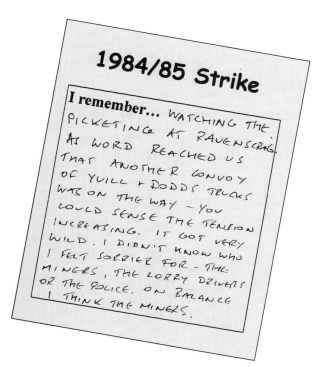

1984/85 Strike

I remember... WATCHING THE PICKETING AT RAVENSCRAIG. AT WORD REACHED US THAT ANOTHER CONVOY OF YUILL + DODDS TRUCKS WAS ON THE WAY — YOU COULD SENSE THE TENSION INCREASING. IT GOT VERY WILD. I DIDN'T KNOW WHO I FELT SORRIER FOR — THE MINERS, THE LORRY DRIVERS OR THE POLICE. ON BALANCE I THINK THE MINERS.

Memories from the exhibition

Members of the public added to the story by writing their memories on comment sheets at the exhibition . . .

The police lost respect because they allowed themselves to be used politically. Four of us travelling to work in Sheffield as television outside broadcast engineers were stopped at police checkpoints, because they thought we were flying pickets.

Community spirit has now been replaced by a consumer society and crass individualism.

Our family lived in Nottingham during the strike. We 'adopted' a striking miner's family and made sure they had enough groceries and household necessities; it gave us a great sense of purpose.

I remember Mick McGahey speaking at Paisley Town Hall. It was packed. He referred to the redundancy packages men were being offered which amounted to two years wages, and he asked 'What they do after that? Eat grass?'

My boat was used for the first floating picket at Cockenzie Power Station. We stopped an oil tanker from getting in to the north pier for over five hours until the police launch from Leith moved us on.

I remember doing the sponsored walk from the Tay Bridge to Methil on the hottest day of a hot summer.

We went to Balmoral to petition the Queen for the reinstatement of victimised miners.

I remember just being married, mortgage etc., coal fire – lovely, until the coal ran out. Got some anthracite, but didn't realise how hot it would be and it burned clean through the bottom of the fire. Oh, happy day!

I would never have managed it without family support.

On several occasions I was in attendance at pits, as a firefighter. The atmosphere was frightening, you felt a mixture of emotions – for the pit workers, the police and the Yuill &

Dodds drivers barricaded in their trucks and forced to drive like madmen.

The sheer feeling of hopelessness.

The French TUC provided a massive amount of Christmas presents; we wrapped them and distributed them to miners' centres throughout Scotland.

Young men led into a dispute that all but the miners knew could not be won.

I remember hairs returning to my kneecaps, clean hands and walking all day in good, healthy, clean air. There may have been some coal production difficulties due to my absence for 377 days!

Scottish Mining Museum

TWENTY YEARS DOWN THE MINES

Fife – The Mining Kingdom
Mining from Kirkintilloch to Clackmannan
& Stirling to Slamannan
Lanarkshire's Mining Legacy
Mining the Lothians
Mining – Ayrshire's Lost Industry
Scotland's Last Days of Colliery Steam
Twenty Years Down the Mines
Yorkshire's Last Days of Colliery Steam

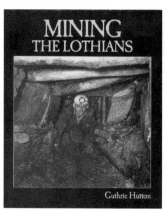

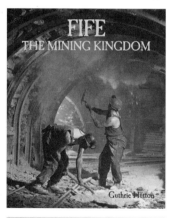

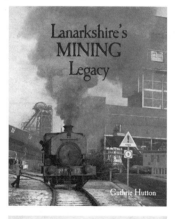

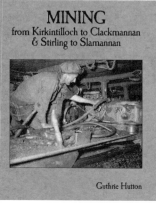

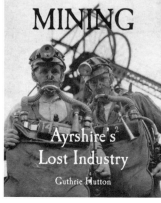